T0064318

LIVING THE
EXCITING LIFE

with
Jesus

MARIE JAN

WESTBOW·
PRESS
A DIVISION OF THOMAS NELSON
& ZONDERVAN

Holy Bible, New Living Translation copyright © 1996, 2004, 2007,
2013 by Tyndale House Foundation. Used by permission of Tyndale
House Publishers Inc., Carol Stream, Illinois 60188. All rights
reserved. New Living, NLT, and the New Living Translation logo
are registered trademarks of Tyndale House Publishers.

WestBow Press books may be ordered through booksellers or by contacting:

WestBow Press
A Division of Thomas Nelson & Zondervan
1663 Liberty Drive
Bloomington, IN 47403
www.westbowpress.com
1 (866) 928-1240

Because of the dynamic nature of the Internet, any web addresses or
links contained in this book may have changed since publication and
may no longer be valid. The views expressed in this work are solely those
of the author and do not necessarily reflect the views of the publisher,
and the publisher hereby disclaims any responsibility for them.

Any people depicted in stock imagery provided by Thinkstock are
models, and such images are being used for illustrative purposes only.
Certain stock imagery © Thinkstock.

ISBN: 978-1-4908-4652-1 (sc)
ISBN: 978-1-4908-4653-8 (e)

Library of Congress Control Number: 2014914239

Printed in the United States of America.

WestBow Press rev. date: 12/10/2014

Contents

INTRODUCTION

This book originated as messages that the Lord shared with me during my private Bible Study. Some of the messages are short. Others are long. These are daily devotionals. Why not write your own thoughts or ideas in the margins as you read a page. Just about every page is a separate thought-provoking topic. They are all about the exciting life of living with Jesus Christ. There may be ups and downs but it is never dull. Please take some time to listen to what the Lord is telling you as you read. He has much to say.

All glory, honor, and praise to our precious Lord and Savior Jesus Christ. Thank you for loving us so much.

Going With the Current

I have been swimming lately. I am not the best swimmer but the lifeguard is very friendly and gives me tips on things to improve. I have been swimming in an indoor facility and staying in the lap portion of the pool. I had seen another part of the pool that was small that appeared to me to be a place where people could go to walk in the water if they wanted. I had not gone over there because I wanted to swim. The lifeguard suggested to me that I try walking in there. So I tried it. It was not at all like I thought. The water is moving in the circular area. Initially I tried walking but the current was pushing me around so quickly that I could not stop moving to put my feet down in this swiftly moving water. Eventually I got my bearings and was able to walk with the current. The lifeguard walked in the vicinity of the area and gave me a thumbs up sign but with a questioningly look. I told her that I loved it. It was quite the challenge. She said if you want a really big challenge, try walking the other way. Then she said but you are not strong enough for that yet. When she said that, I felt compelled to try it. I did eventually make it around that circle walking against the current. It was incredibly difficult for me.

Interestingly, I found that the hardest place to change directions is at the point where the current is moving fastest. As the current is weakest at the entry point and strongest at the departure point which is essentially the same place. At that point it is much easier to go the way of the current than to push against it and go the other direction. You have to decide if you are going to go the direction that propels you forward or go against the current where you are fighting for each step that you take. The distance around the circle remains the same but walking around it takes at least three times longer when going against the water.

For Christians, it may be easier to go along with the world and walk in the direction of the current. If we do this, we are just fitting in and we lose our flavor. (Matthew 5:13 New Living Translation "You are the salt of the earth. But what good is salt if it has lost its flavor? Can you make it salty again? It will be thrown out and trampled underfoot as worthless.) If we make an effort to fit in with everyone what difference are we making for the body of Christ. If we decide to take the path that the Lord has established for us, it is likely that our path will be more difficult. We will not fit in with the world. In fact, we will stand out in a way that may not be comfortable. As believers we have been given directions. The question is, are we willing to go against the current in order to follow them?

Matthew 28:18-20 NLT Jesus came and told his disciples, "I have been given all authority in heaven and on earth. 19 Therefore, go and make disciples of all the nations, baptizing them in the name of the Father and the Son and the Holy Spirit. 20 Teach these new disciples to obey all the commands I have given you. And be sure of this: I am with you always, even to the end of the age."

PEACE OF MIND

Mark 9:2-8 Six days later Jesus took Peter, James, and John, and led them up a high mountain to be alone. As the men watched, Jesus' appearance was transformed, 3 and his clothes became dazzling white, far whiter than any earthly bleach could ever make them. 4 Then Elijah and Moses appeared and began talking with Jesus. 5 Peter exclaimed, "Rabbi, it's wonderful for us to be here! Let's make three shelters as memorials—one for you, one for Moses, and one for Elijah." 6 He said this because he didn't really know what else to say, for they were all terrified.7 Then a cloud overshadowed them, and a voice from the cloud said, "This is my dearly loved Son. Listen to him." 8 Suddenly, when they looked around, Moses and Elijah were gone, and they saw only Jesus with them. When reading this scripture there could be the tendency to ask, why didn't Peter just keep quiet. Jesus had allowed Peter, James and John to see this wonderful miracle, nothing that they could fathom on their own. Then Peter starts talking. It says in verse 6 that they were all terrified. I can imagine that it would be even more terrifying when a cloud settled right over them and a voice spoke, "This is my dearly loved Son listen to Him." That was God's kind and loving way of telling Peter to hush.

I must admit that if I take a sincere introspective look at myself, I might have started talking just like Peter. Being scared can bring about some actions in which we would not normally engage. Sometimes life feels scary. Illness, bereavement, divorce, disappointments of all kinds may promote a scary feeling. At times, even as believers, we may feel so distraught that we cannot seem to think straight. We are looking for answers and can't find any. At those times if at all possible, go to a quiet space with a mind set on prayer, reading of the Bible, and a mind and heart attuned to God to hear what He is saying. He may or may not answer our questions. But He may remind us that He is with us, that He provides peace in a storm, and that He loves us with an incomparable love. There are times when we need to be quiet so that we may hear what the Lord is saying.

John 14:27 "I am leaving you with a gift—peace of mind and heart. And the peace I give is a gift the world cannot give. So don't be troubled or afraid.

Psalm 107:28-30 "Lord, help!" they cried in their trouble, and he saved them from their distress. 29 He calmed the storm to a whisper and stilled the waves.

GOD FIGHTS OUR BATTLES

Psalm 54

1 Come with great power, O God, and rescue me! Defend me with your might.

2 Listen to my prayer, O God. Pay attention to my plea.

3 For strangers are attacking me; violent people are trying to kill me. They care nothing for God. Interlude

4 But God is my helper. The Lord keeps me alive!

5 May the evil plans of my enemies be turned against them. Do as you promised and put an end to them.

6 I will sacrifice a voluntary offering to you; I will praise your name, O Lord, for it is good.

7 For you have rescued me from my troubles and helped me to triumph over my enemies.

In this Psalm, the psalmist is David. He is speaking about a time when people advised Saul of David's location. Saul sought to kill David. He was jealous of David. (1 Samuel 18:9 So from that time on Saul kept a jealous eye on David.)

We see that David is asking the Lord to defend him. Despite David's victorious fight against Goliath and many other triumphs, David knew that the Lord was the one who was fighting the battles. (1 Samuel 17:47 And everyone assembled here will know that the Lord rescues his people, but not with sword and spear. This is the Lord's battle, and he will give you to us!")

With the knowledge that God fights our battles, David entreats the Lord for help. Even though the Lord knows the situation that David faces, David still takes the time to tell God about his concern and ask God for His help. Only God has the power to turn the evil plans of our enemies against them. David is confident in his request as he has the expectation of the Lord answering him. This expectation is not based on God owing David or anybody else. David faithfully petitions God because of who God is and the promises that the Lord has made regarding His children. We, too may faithfully and confidently petition God with our requests.

Matthew 7:8 For everyone who asks, receives. Everyone who seeks, finds. And to everyone who knocks, the door will be opened.

SETTING A TRAP

Proverbs 26:27 If you set a trap for others, you will get caught in it yourself. If you roll a boulder down on others, it will crush you instead.

Some things are hard to admit to ourselves. Do we ever have such hostile feelings toward another that we set up traps for them? We probably would not think of it consciously in those words, but if we are planning something with the intention of it being to the detriment of others, we are setting a trap for them.

This evening I was watching a program on a cable channel where a team is brought in at the request of the owner. The nature of the show is that the store owner or manager is having a problem with disappearing funds, supplies, employee infighting or any other number of problems. On this particular episode there was a woman who had been the employee of the month for four months in a row. The owner was very impressed by her. She was also very impressed by herself as she bragged a lot and also tattled a lot to the manager, much like a child.

The team that goes in undercover has the whole restaurant set up with microphones and cameras so that any and everything that the employees do is seen on camera. Much to the disgust of the owner, the reason for the employee's consistent wins as employee of the month was that she was sabotaging other employees. She would change or throw away orders that came in from the other wait staff making them look incompetent. She flattered the manager, telling him that he looked good and it appeared that he had been working out. At one point she even told one of her co-workers what a beautiful shirt that she was wearing. Then she went to the back to tell the manager that one of the customers had complained about how low cut the woman's top was, which was untrue. A different employee was threatened with the possibility of being fired due to this server's underhanded methods. But the camera showed all the devious things she was doing.

Initially, she was fired, but the owner responded to her begging request to be reinstated and promises to stop her underhanded methods. She had a set a trap for others but ended up getting caught in it herself. She rolled a boulder to knock down others but ended up getting knocked over by it herself.

If we seek God's will and direction, we will receive whatever He has for us. We do not need to create schemes and set traps in order to progress.

Matthew 6:33 Seek the Kingdom of God above all else, and live righteously, and he will give you everything you need.

POURED OUT LOVE

Psalm 42:8-11 But each day the Lord pours his unfailing love upon me, and through each night I sing his songs, praying to God who gives me life.

9 "O God my rock," I cry, "Why have you forgotten me? Why must I wander around in grief, oppressed by my enemies?"

10 Their taunts break my bones.They scoff, "Where is this God of yours?"

11 Why am I discouraged? Why is my heart so sad? I will put my hope in God! I will praise him again— my Savior and my God!

The first thing that is brought to our attention in this passage is that the Lord pours His unfailing love on us. It does not say that He drizzles out His love, but He pours it! Thank you Lord!

The psalmist then talks about singing songs and praying to God, who gives us life. But the psalmist also openly shares his feelings to the Lord; crying out to the Lord and asking why have you forgotten about me? Why are you allowing my enemies to treat me this way? Their insults hurt me so much! They are even making fun of you, Lord!

In verse 11, it is as if the psalmist started remembering who was available to help him. He begins to question his own discouragement and sadness when he remembers that He can place his hope in God. He remembers the Lord and decides to praise Him. He alone is our Savior and our God.

Don't Be Afraid

Joshua 1:9 This is my command—be strong and courageous! Do not be afraid or discouraged. For the Lord your God is with you wherever you go."

This scripture passage is very encouraging. God in His great wisdom knew that we would face moments of discouragement on this earth. Truly if we talk with other believers we find that many are facing trials and tribulations that have the potential to be quite discouraging. But God gives us a message to hold on to in these difficult times. It brings to mind a person trying to stay afloat in water, they are struggling and the water is deep. That person called for help and it seemed that no one could reach them. But just when that person believes they are going to sink, someone throws them a lifeline, be it a rope or a small rescue boat, the one who was about to give up not only was removed from a point of discouragement but progressed to a point of encouragement. They were not alone out there on the waters. Someone saw their predicament and found a way to lend a hand.

Our precious Lord is sending us a lifeline in this passage of scripture. We need not be afraid or discouraged. We are not alone. The Lord is with us wherever we go.

By His Spirit

Zechariah 4:6-8

6 Then he said to me, "This is what the Lord says to Zerubbabel: It is not by force nor by strength, but by my Spirit, says the Lord of Heaven's Armies. 7 Nothing, not even a mighty mountain, will stand in Zerubbabel's way; it will become a level plain before him! And when Zerubbabel sets the final stone of the Temple in place, the people will shout: 'May God bless it! May God bless it!'

In this passage, the Lord is speaking to Zechariah. The Lord is telling Zechariah the message that He has for Zerubbabel. From verse 6 - It is not by force, not by strength but by His Spirit - that the work will be accomplished. In the verses following verse 6 the Lord continues to talk about what He will do to help Zerubbabel. After those things are done, the people will be shouting - May God bless it.

When we read this scripture it puts me in the mindset of times when it seemed that I was banging my head against the wall every time I tried to work through a situation. I kept trying to fix it and my fixes did not work. But we see in this passage that the Lord is saying, not by force or strength but by the Spirit of God will this thing be accomplished. This thought is critical for us to understand. In circumstances when God tells us what to do in order to address a situation, the reason that it is successful is because of God's Spirit. In this passage we see that once the work is accomplished the people will be looking to the Lord to bless it. So despite the fact that God is using Zerubbabel, the focus of the people remains on the Lord. Likewise, whatever Godly thing that we achieve, we must recognize that it was achieved by the Spirit of the Lord. God should always receive the glory. The focus should be on Him.

WHO CAN BE AGAINST US

Romans 8:31-34

31 What shall we say about such wonderful things as these? If God is for us, who can ever be against us? 32 Since he did not spare even his own Son but gave him up for us all, won't he also give us everything else? 33 Who dares accuse us whom God has chosen for his own? No one—for God himself has given us right standing with himself. 34 Who then will condemn us? No one—for Christ Jesus died for us and was raised to life for us, and he is sitting in the place of honor at God's right hand, pleading for us.

The Word of God says who can be against us; who can accuse us since God is for us? God himself gave us right standing with Him.

(2 Corinthians 5:21 For God made Christ, who never sinned, to be the offering for our sin, so that we could be made right with God through Christ.)

This is all related to a walk of faith. The same faith that we stand on when we proclaim our salvation based on - Romans 10:9 If you openly declare that Jesus is Lord and believe in your heart that God raised him from the dead, you will be saved.- is the same faith that we utilize to believe that no can be against us or accuse us. At times it does seem that we are being accused and that many are against us. But the great lengths that the Lord took to enable us to have a right relationship with Him and the fact that Jesus is sitting in the place of honor at God's right hand pleading for us, says that we must stand on faith and not what we see. Will we believe what our eyes tell us and our ears hear or will we boldly stand on the Word of God?We are not the reason for this release from accusation. It is God himself who provided it. We must stand on the Word of God!

Overflowing Love

1 Thessalonians 3:12-13 12 And may the Lord make your love for one another and for all people grow and overflow, just as our love for you overflows. 13 May he, as a result, make your hearts strong, blameless, and holy as you stand before God our Father when our Lord Jesus comes again with all his holy people. Amen.

This scripture passage is written by Paul, Silas and Timothy to the church of Thessalonica. They are encouraging the church to grow their love for one another and for all people. They are asking that the Lord make their hearts strong, blameless and holy as a result of that great love for others.

That is a good prayer for all, that our love would increase for others in the body of Christ and for all people. If our love for one another and other believers grows, what would we do differently? Have we ever seen a person that seems to be consistently disagreeable? Have we observed a change in that person when someone that they truly love comes around? Often their eyes light up, a slow smile spreads across their face and their tone and even the inflections in their voice soften.

Interestingly, if our love grows for everyone in the church and for all people, that means we would love everybody. That sounds good, but is a challenging concept to pursue and live out in our lives. We would probably not run to every person that crossed our paths with a resounding, I love you. But love would change our actions. A change in our actions would speak much more loudly than telling everyone that we loved them.

In our world today, people are often out for themselves alone. Some focus solely on their wants and goals so much that anything that falls out of the realm of their desire is of uninterest to them. If their desire to achieve something kills someone else's dreams or harms another significantly, they do not care. This is definitely not a Godly way. When our love for others grows, one way that we notice it in ourselves is that we consider the impact of what we do to other people. This does not mean that we spend our lives trying to please everybody else, it means we continue in our efforts to please God by caring about His children and His creations.

JESUS DID IT FOR US

Matthew 27:27-31 Some of the governor's soldiers took Jesus into their headquarters and called out the entire regiment. 28 They stripped him and put a scarlet robe on him. 29 They wove thorn branches into a crown and put it on his head, and they placed a reed stick in his right hand as a scepter. Then they knelt before him in mockery and taunted, "Hail! King of the Jews!" 30 And they spit on him and grabbed the stick and struck him on the head with it. 31 When they were finally tired of mocking him, they took off the robe and put his own clothes on him again. Then they led him away to be crucified.

So often when we speak about the sacrifice that Jesus made for us, we focus on the stripes that he took, being struck with a lead-tipped whip, the nails that were driven into his body and when He carried our sins on the cross. But that is not all that He experienced.

After Jesus was whipped, Jesus had to face an entire regiment of the governor's soldiers. How humiliating when they stripped Him and then put a scarlet robe on Him in great insincerity. Have you ever been working in a garden and fallen into a tree with thorns or been trimming a bush that has thorns and felt the pain of one thorn? It hurts. But some of the men from the governor's regiment wove a crown of thorns for Jesus. Even with my limited knowledge regarding weaving, I know that you cannot weave with only one piece of string. Likewise, they would have to have at least 2-3 branches of thorns to weave together a "crown" for Jesus. These men were so cruel and Jesus was suffering before they even headed to the cross. They mockingly worshipped Jesus. They spit on him. They spit on our Savior. How offended would we be if one, let alone several, people spit on us?

Could Jesus have left and said I am going back to my Father, I do not have to put up with this? Yes, He could have. But He stayed there and allowed them to treat him so horribly because of His love for us. Thank you Jesus! Praise your name! Thank you for accepting such horrific humiliation and torture for us. We did not and do not deserve your goodness and love, but you gave it to us anyway. Thank you so much Jesus!

SEEK THE KINGDOM FIRST

Acts 2:42-47 All the believers devoted themselves to the apostles' teaching, and to fellowship, and to sharing in meals (including the Lord's Supper, and to prayer.

43 A deep sense of awe came over them all, and the apostles performed many miraculous signs and wonders. 44 And all the believers met together in one place and shared everything they had. 45 They sold their property and possessions and shared the money with those in need. 46 They worshiped together at the Temple each day, met in homes for the Lord's Supper, and shared their meals with great joy and generosity— 47 all the while praising God and enjoying the goodwill of all the people. And each day the Lord added to their fellowship those who were being saved.

At this time in scripture, Jesus had been crucified and had arisen. He ascended to the Father and came back with instructions on what to do. He told them that He needed to leave in order to receive the Holy Spirit. So Jesus had left again but promised that He would return again one day - the day that we believers long for - to be united with Christ in Heaven. The Holy Spirit had come. Many had received the Holy Spirit.

In today's scripture passage, believers devoted themselves to the apostles' teaching, fellowship and sharing meals, including the Lord's supper and prayer. The word devoted means to concentrate on a particular pursuit or purpose. The believers were devoted to doing, following and learning about the things of Christ.

The apostles performed many signs and wonders as Jesus had prophesied. (John 14:12 "I tell you the truth, anyone who believes in me will do the same works I have done, and even greater works, because I am going to be with the Father.) The people met together and shared everything they had. They worshipped together every day, praising God and sharing with great generosity. The Lord added to their fellowship with additional people being saved.

What are we focused on? Do we make an effort to attend church or have we minimized worshipping together to a religious routine or chore? Are we excited about learning? I have heard people say that they had already read the Bible so why did they need to study anymore. (Yes, they were serious.)

Generosity, some people cringe at the word. Yet in this passage of scripture and in various places in the Bible it tells us to share with those in need. Everything that we have was provided to us at the hand of God so technically it is really His. Do we give away all of our food, clothing, money and goods or do we recognize the needs of others and help in the way in which God directs? I believe we are to follow the latter. Are we willing to follow the example of the believers in today's scripture passage? It is time for us all to prioritize and put Jesus first.

Matthew 6:33 Seek the Kingdom of God above all else, and live righteously, and he will give you everything you need.

THANKSGIVING AND PRAISE

Luke 8:1-3 Soon afterward Jesus began a tour of the nearby towns and villages, preaching and announcing the Good News about the Kingdom of God. He took his twelve disciples with him, 2 along with some women who had been cured of evil spirits and diseases. Among them were Mary Magdalene, from whom he had cast out seven demons; 3 Joanna, the wife of Chuza, Herod's business manager; Susanna; and many others who were contributing from their own resources to support Jesus and his disciples.

During the time of Jesus' ministry, he spent much time preaching and announcing the news. Many are aware that he took his disciples with him but conceivably fewer know that some women who had been cured of evil spirits and diseases also accompanied Him. In the four gospels, the book of Luke includes the most information about the women who were in support of Jesus' ministry.

However, for purposes of this lesson, the gender of the people that accompanied Jesus and His disciples is not particularly relevant. What is relevant is that once they received from God, they sought to remain in His presence. How many people are elated when they receive salvation but have no desire to dig deeper into the full knowledge of Christ. How many of us have a deep desire to be in His presence - be it at home study, worshipping with the body of Christ or in prayer and thanksgiving. Do we want to get to know the Savior of our souls a little better? The breadth and width of His love, wisdom and guidance is immeasurable.

Do we desire to draw near to the one who gave His life for us? He took the punishment that should have been our's. Does that prompt us to want to get to know Him better? Prayerfully, He has that impact on all of us. How do we go about getting a greater knowledge of Him? We get this knowledge and closer relationship with Christ by studying the Bible, worshipping with the saints,spending time in prayer, communication with God, and through praise and thanksgiving

Psalm 100:4 Enter his gates with thanksgiving; go into his courts with praise. Give thanks to him and praise his name.

Pray And Don't Give Up

Luke 18:1-8 One day Jesus told his disciples a story to show that they should always pray and never give up. 2 "There was a judge in a certain city," he said, "who neither feared God nor cared about people. 3 A widow of that city came to him repeatedly, saying, 'Give me justice in this dispute with my enemy.' 4 The judge ignored her for a while, but finally he said to himself, 'I don't fear God or care about people, 5 but this woman is driving me crazy. I'm going to see that she gets justice, because she is wearing me out with her constant requests!'"

6 Then the Lord said, "Learn a lesson from this unjust judge. 7 Even he rendered a just decision in the end. So don't you think God will surely give justice to his chosen people who cry out to him day and night? Will he keep putting them off? 8 I tell you, he will grant justice to them quickly! But when the Son of Man returns, how many will he find on the earth who have faith?"

In verse 8 of the chapter above, the latter part of that verse asks,'How many many will the Son of Man find who have faith?'

Hebrews 11:1 tells us what faith is, but knowing what it is and having it are different. (Hebrews 11:1 Faith is the confidence that what we hope for will actually happen; it gives us assurance about things we cannot see.)

Jesus, in the parable/story above, is providing His disciples with the awareness that we should never give up and that we should always pray. Prayer is one type of evidence of faith.

Why would we pray to the Lord if we did not think He could do anything?

This parable talks about a judge who does not care about people. Can you imagine, the person who is deciding your case not having any interest or care about you or what happens to you? The judge decides to ignore the woman in this case. Little did he know that the woman was going to come back repeatedly seeking justice. I can imagine that each time she came back he would think, 'here comes that old woman again. Well she is going to get a big disappointment if she thinks that I am going to pay her any attention.' But at some point this judge, who could care less about people got tired of seeing this woman and said "OK, I find in your favor."

Now that unjust judge eventually gave the woman justice because she was driving him crazy. With that knowledge would we not know that our just God would provide justice to us when we cry out to Him day and night?

If you feel like giving up, if you feel disregarded because you have not received a resolution to the issue in which you are praying - hold on! Stand in faith! We serve a just God who cares about His children. (Psalm 139:17-18 How precious are your thoughts about me, O God. They cannot be numbered! 18 I can't even count them; they outnumber the grains of sand! And when I wake up, you are still with me!

Psalm 50:14-15 Make thankfulness your sacrifice to God, and keep the vows you made to the Most High. 15 Then call on me when you are in trouble, and I will rescue you, and you will give me glory.")

Humility

Ephesians 4:2-3

2 Always be humble and gentle. Be patient with each other, making allowance for each other's faults because of your love. 3 Make every effort to keep yourselves united in the Spirit, binding yourselves together with peace.

Throughout the Bible we find numerous scriptures about the ways that we should interact with each other. The repetition of these instructions strongly suggests that it is extremely important to God that we treat other believers and nonbelievers in a Godly fashion.

Always be humble and gentle. That is somewhat challenging as it does not say when convenient, or once in a while; it says always. To be humble is to not be proud or arrogant; to be modest or low in rank, importance, status. When we are humble, we do not look down on other people. When we are humble we do not disregard another person because "they have not achieved our level of greatness." Please note that the last statement is written facetiously, as no one is great but the Lord. If anyone has done anything that is perceived to be great, all the glory continues to belong to the Lord. Who gave us mouths to speak, tongues that move and allow us to enunciate words, a mind that can understand and a heart that provides the ability to love graciously. Everything we are able to do is given to us by God, so there is no room for pride, only humility and gratefulness.

Always be gentle; not severe, rough or violent. Are we gentle when we address others? (Proverbs 15:1 A gentle answer deflects anger, but harsh words make tempers flare.) Since scriptures tells us that harsh words cause anger, when it is possible we should wait to interact with others if we cannot address others in the way that God has said.

We are to be patient with one another and to bind together in peace. Something that can easily be forgotten by all, is that patience is not a challenge in calm, easygoing situations or around pleasant, calm people. Patience, an ability or willingness to suppress restlessness or annoyance when confronted with delay, is challenging in difficult situations and with people whom we do not enjoy interacting. There is the necessity of a lack of confusion in order for us to be bound together in peace. (1 Corinthians 14:33 For God is not a God of disorder but of peace, as in all the meetings of God's holy people.) Being peaceful may be easy or difficult depending on the situation. We must remember that God does not ask us to do anything that He has not empowered us to do. So when we are having difficulties doing things the way that He said, we need only to pray and ask Him for help. Interestingly, we may find that God seemingly leaves the situation the same and simply makes changes in us.

GUIDE MY FEET BY THE LIGHT

Matthew 24:4-14

4 Jesus told them, "Don't let anyone mislead you, 5 for many will come in my name, claiming, 'I am the Messiah.' They will deceive many. 6 And you will hear of wars and threats of wars, but don't panic. Yes, these things must take place, but the end won't follow immediately. 7 Nation will go to war against nation, and kingdom against kingdom. There will be famines and earthquakes in many parts of the world. 8 But all this is only the first of the birth pains, with more to come.

Lately, there has been much talk about the end times. In verse 4, we see where it says that there will be people who tried to mislead you,coming in the name of Christ. One that I still remember is the Jonestown Massacre from 1978. There was a man named Jim Jones who started a "church" in 1956 called the people's temple.It was in operation for over 20 years. People were fooled by his lies and eventually were led into a forced mass suicide. Over 900 people died in one day.

The Bible is the Word of God. When we familiarize ourselves with it, we are less likely to be misled. We will also be able to identify when what is being taught is accurate or not. Some are misled because what they initially hear is true. Then if close attention is paid, the teachings change to being partially true. By the time it is obvious that the teachings are totally incorrect some people are so involved in an occult or fake church that they do not know how to get out.

The wars and threats of wars has been happening for a while now, but the Word of God says that these things will happen but it will still not be the time of the end. Nations and kindgoms fighting each other was, is and based on the Bible will continue to happen. Have we noticed the incredible number of famines and earthquakes all over the world?. These things are happening now, but the Bible says that these are just the beginnings of the birth pains to come. Have you ever seen a woman in labor? The first contractions come and the woman is very uncomfortable. As the contractions become more frequent and more intense the uncomfortable feeling becomes intense pain. Jesus explains that the things mentioned in this scripture passage are just the beginning of the birth pains. To continue with this analogy, the intense labor has yet to come.

(Psalm 119:105 Your word is a lamp to guide my feet and a light for my path.) Without the Word of God, we will be walking without light with no guide. We need to study the Word.

Always Be Honorable

2 Corinthians 4:1-2 Therefore, since God in his mercy has given us this new way,we never give up. 2 We reject all shameful deeds and underhanded methods. We don't try to trick anyone or distort the word of God. We tell the truth before God, and all who are honest know this.

The apostle Paul is speaking in the above passage to the church in Corinth. Although Paul was addressing that church specifically, the words are just as relevant for the church today. The old way was the law. The new way is grace, unmerited favor. Yet even with this new way, Paul is reminding them to never give up regardless of the circumstance.

We do not give up and we also do not do sneaky or underhanded things in order to achieve what we want. Do we buy things knowing that the items were obtained in an improper way, such as theft. I remember being over a friend's house once and they asked if I wanted to watch a movie, to which I said, "Sure". When they put in the movie I wondered why the picture quality was so bad and I hadn't thought that the movie was out on tape (this occurred a while ago, so there were no DVDs yet). As I continued to watch the movie, in the middle of one scene the picture was blocked for a while as a person walked in front of and blocked the camera. Then I realized what I was watching. It was truly the movie but someone had sneaked a camera into the theatre so that they could tape and then sell the movie. This may sound like a small thing. But if we were to ask the director, the actors, the make-up artists, the producers, etc that were not getting paid because of the underhanded method of the individual who taped the movie and also the ones who bought it- they would probably consider it a big deal. Some ungodly things would not prosper if people stopped supporting them. And as Godly people, we really have no business supporting underhanded things. As we remember, Paul's message in this passage is given to the church not unbelievers.

There are times when we have done things that we did not consider underhanded. But if we ask God to show us some things that we are doing or have done that are displeasing or displeased Him, we may find that we need to change some things. God is forgiving. We can repent and start over. Let us honor God in all of our ways.

Psalm 119:33-37

33 Teach me your decrees, O Lord; I will keep them to the end.

34 Give me understanding and I will obey your instructions; I will put them into practice with all my heart.

35 Make me walk along the path of your commands, for that is where my happiness is found.

36 Give me an eagerness for your laws rather than a love for money!

37 Turn my eyes from worthless things, and give me life through your word.

SEE HIS FACE

Psalm 11:4-7 But the Lord is in his holy Temple; the Lord still rules from heaven. He watches everyone closely, examining every person on earth. 5 The Lord examines both the righteous and the wicked. He hates those who love violence. 6 He will rain down blazing coals and burning sulfur on the wicked, punishing them with scorching winds.7 For the righteous Lord loves justice.The virtuous will see his face.

When we watch local or network news the stories can be both saddening and sickening at the same time. The phrase 'Man's inhumanity to Man' originated in a poem by Robert Burns. But to see those words in action, we can watch the news, hear stories from another, and at other times actually witness it with our own eyes. People have asked, if God is so good why would He allow these awful things to happen? One scripture in particular speaks not of a probability of tribulation or difficulties but speaks with certainty of it when we live on this earth.(John 16:33 I have told you all this so that you may have peace in me. Here on earth you will have many trials and sorrows. But take heart, because I have overcome the world.") Another passage that speaks to this issue is (1 Peter 5:8 Stay alert! Watch out for your great enemy, the devil. He prowls around like a roaring lion, looking for someone to devour.) The devil is going around like a lion seeking whom he may devour. But unlike the lion who actually does devour its prey once caught, the devil is only like a lion as he seeks to devour. If you are familiar with the book of Job, particularly Job 1:6-12, you will see that satan has to ask God's permission before he does anything. God does allow hardships but even hardships work together for the good of those who love the Lord and are called according to His purpose for them. (Romans 8:28).

Our scripture passage today assures us that God is not unaware of what is taking place on the earth. He examines everyone closely, the righteous and the wicked. He hates violence and will punish those who perpetuate it. Some people may feel as if they have successfully gotten away with something because no other human being saw them or caught them. But they are incorrect. God sees and will punish those who are violent and wicked as noted in verse 6 of Psalm 11. Those who are virtuous, followers of God, will one day see His face.

Galatians 6:9 So let's not get tired of doing what is good. At just the right time we will reap a harvest of blessing if we don't give up.

STAY AWAY FROM EVIL

Proverbs 4:14-18 Don't do as the wicked do, and don't follow the path of evildoers. 15 Don't even think about it; don't go that way. Turn away and keep moving. 16 For evil people can't sleep until they've done their evil deed for the day. They can't rest until they've caused someone to stumble. 17 They eat the food of wickedness and drink the wine of violence! 18 The way of the righteous is like the first gleam of dawn, which shines ever brighter until the full light of day.

Believers are not to do the things that wicked people do. One might think, 'well of course, that's pretty obvious'. Interestingly enough, it is not as obvious as we might think. Often when we see a depiction of the devil, he is in a bright red suit with horns. Just about all believers would run away from the enemy if he looked like that. Instead he studies us in an effort to present himself to us in a way that we would find appealing.

The wickedness that the devil initiates could be compared to a boa constrictor. They wear some of the most distinctive markings of all reptiles. The markings are dependent on the habitat they are trying to blend into- so they do not stand out and the approaching danger is not obvious. Their jaws are lined with small, hooked teeth for grabbing and holding prey while they wrap their muscular bodies around their victim, squeezing until it suffocates. The constrictor, like wickedness, gets our interest in something and then hooks onto us. It is not until then that it begins to squeeze.

When people who consistently involve themselves in wicked acts try to pull us in, it generally starts with something small. We may even feel in our spirit that something is wrong but we think that it is really no big deal. Eventually the nature of the evil activities escalates and we may feel trapped. But all praise to God, feeling trapped is indeed just a feeling. The Lord has promised a way of escape. (1 Corinthians 10:13 The temptations in your life are no different from what others experience. And God is faithful. He will not allow the temptation to be more than you can stand. When you are tempted, he will show you a way out so that you can endure.)

The better way is to follow the direction of the scripture passage noted a the beginning of the page - Proverbs 4:14-15 Don't do as the wicked do, and don't follow the path of evildoers. 15 Don't even think about it; don't go that way. Turn away and keep moving.

No Deceit

1 Peter 2:1-3 So get rid of all evil behavior. Be done with all deceit, hypocrisy, jealousy, and all unkind speech. 2 Like newborn babies, you must crave pure spiritual milk so that you will grow into a full experience of salvation. Cry out for this nourishment, 3 now that you have had a taste of the Lord's kindness.

Verse 1 in the above passage is rich with guidance on how a believer should live. Get rid of all evil behavior. Do we as believers do any evil things? If we are doing ungodly things or doing things with hate in our hearts, yes we are participating in evil behavior. We are to be done with all deception. Are we done with deceit? Have we said in our hearts, "I really did not lie, I just did not tell them everything"? It is likely that if we had not left out a particular part the person's perception would have been totally different. If that is the case, we are practicing deceit in that situation. Hypocrisy, do we act one way around some people and act differently around others, even behaving in the manner that we supposedly find despicable according to what we have said to one group of people. Do we do that and do we think that God is OK with that? The Lord says to be done with hypocrisy. Be who we are wherever we are. Jealousy. Do we have great disdain for an individual because they are more successful than we are? Are we irritated by the house and/or car that they drive? Do we find that they have a great looking spouse and our's is just sort of plain? We would probably not voice this feeling to anyone but if we feel this way, it sounds as though we have issues with jealousy. The Lord says to be done with all unkind speech. That is pretty straight-forward but at times easier said than done. When someone almost runs us off the road because they are in such a hurry, what word or type of words come from our mouths? When we see someone's apparel and we find it to be substandard in our eyes, are our words unkind? Truly there is a way to address matters in kind fashion or in an evil way. Which way do we use?Might we be deceitful and hypocritical and comment on things one way with one person and a completely opposite way with another.

If we needed to sum up this passage, I believe the Lord would tell us to keep our focus on Him. Would our words be pleasing or displeasing to Him? What we speak about says a lot about us. (Matthew 15:19 For from the heart come evil thoughts, murder, adultery, all sexual immorality, theft, lying, and slander.

Matthew 6:21 Wherever your treasure is, there the desires of your heart will also be.)

PERFECT PEACE

Isaiah 26:3-4,8 You will keep in perfect peace all who trust in you, all whose thoughts are fixed on you! 4 Trust in the Lord always, for the Lord God is the eternal Rock.

8 Lord, we show our trust in you by obeying your laws; our heart's desire is to glorify your name.

God gives peace to His children. Are all of God's children in situations that would be considered peaceful? We only need to watch the news or have a conversation with another believer in order to know that many are in non-peaceful situations. The word says that God will keep in perfect peace all who trust in him. So during these days of unbelievable trials and circumstances, God offers the opportunity for peace. The Lord says that we will have peace if we trust in Him. When we trust Him we remember the awesomeness of the one to whom we trust and know that regardless of the situation He is still in charge and He is working in the midst of it all - whether we see it or not. Verse 4 makes it so plain for us: Trust in the Lord always, for the Lord God is the eternal Rock.

What can we do in response to the loving promises that we just read? Verse 8 says that we show our trust by being obedient to the Lord's laws so that He may be glorified. The Word does not say that we gain salvation by obeying His laws. It says that we show our trust by obeying His laws as our hearts desire is to glorify His name. Obeying His laws not only shows our trust but it helps us in whatever situation we face. The Almighty, All-Knowing

God has given us guidelines identifying how to live and how to address situations in our lives. When we follow the route that the Almighty God has established rather than our own ways, we are setting ourselves up to be blessed. When we decide to follow a different way than God's way, we are setting ourselves up for difficulty and failure. Blessed be the name of the Lord.

Amazing Lord

Isaiah 40:12-14 Who else has held the oceans in his hand? Who has measured off the heavens with his fingers? Who else knows the weight of the earth or has weighed the mountains and hills on a scale?

13 Who is able to advise the Spirit of the Lord? Who knows enough to give him advice or teach him?

14 Has the Lord ever needed anyone's advice? Does he need instruction about what is good? Did someone teach him what is right or show him the path of justice?

Do we truly consider with whom it is that we are allowed to speak and with whom it is that actually desires to hear from and speak with us? If we received an invitation from the president of the company where we are employed, would we be impressed and share the news with others. If the mayor or governor or other important official was having a dinner and provided us with an invitation, tickets and an offer to sit at their specific table would we think,'Wow, we must be doing something right to get that invitation.' Yet we have an invitation to not only be saved by, but to develop a relationship with the creator and Savior of the world. How do we respond?

Have we ever been on the ocean shore and looked across the waters to see nothing but more water and the sky? According to the above passage of scripture the Lord has held the oceans in His hand. That is awe inspiring. Have we ever pondered the weight of the earth? Even if we had not before, when we consider the oceans, the mountains, the valleys, the trees, the land mass, and various other miscellaneous and sundry things; we can only guess the weight of the world or obtain a scientific approximation. God knows the weight of the earth. He is truly amazing! He is without compare!

Our Lord provides us with an open invitation to salvation. He provides us with an endless invite for communication. Are we in awe of His greatness and the fact that He wants to spend time with us? There is no other request of greater significance than the ones that come from the Lord. Will we answer and spend time with Him today?

JESUS SERVED

Luke 22:27

Who is more important, the one who sits at the table or the one who serves? The one who sits at the table, of course. But not here! For I am among you as one who serves.

Jesus is speaking in the above passage. He lowered Himself for our benefit. (Philippians 2:5-8 You must have the same attitude that Christ Jesus had. 6 Though he was God, he did not think of equality with God as something to cling to. 7 Instead, he gave up his divine privileges; he took the humble position of a slave and was born as a human being. When he appeared in human form, 8 he humbled himself in obedience to God and died a criminal's death on a cross.)

There is so much work to be done for Christ. There are times when God has shown us a specific need in the body of Christ. We see the need and choose not to address it because it takes us out of our comfort zone, we have an enjoyable commitment that might be endangered if we offer to help, we are afraid that people will start asking us to do everything, and sadly, at times we really do not care. There are innumerable reasons why we choose to not do things for the Lord. We may not be thinking about them consciously as a refusal to do some work for Christ, but at times we are following that old saying, "You only live once." This could be used as a rationale not to do many things because there is so much to do in this world and we do not want to miss out on it. We have not yet achieved all of the things on our "bucket list." All people only live once. So if we do not take the time to share the Good News, some may live eternally in Hell in eternal damnation.

Jesus set the ultimate example. (Philippians 2:5-8) Can you imagine being in a place of no sin, sorrow, or sadness? He, being God came down to earth and did not take a position of importance which would have been rightfully His. Jesus came down to earth to serve. He took a servant's position and died a criminal's death. Could anything be more humbling than that? He did this so that we could have eternal life with Him.

Let us look for opportunities to serve, opportunities in which to humble ourselves that we may follow the example of our Lord.

LOVE COVERS OFFENSES

How do we treat one another?

Psalm 69:8 Even my own brothers pretend they don't know me; they treat me like a stranger.

This scripture passage from the psalmist sounds pretty serious. Can we imagine our siblings acting like they do not know us, treating us like strangers? This may be more common than we would imagine. When we get to know people we sometimes hear about "that" family member that everyone else hopes does not show up for a gathering. Even in our own families, we may be able to think of at least one whose arrival is met with loud sights or eye rolls and their departure is met with unspoken (or spoken) delight.

Usually there is what one would consider a legitimate reason for this. Even the proverbs speaks of those to whom we should stay away. (Proverbs 22:24-25 Don't befriend angry people or associate with hot-tempered people, 25 or you will learn to be like them and endanger your soul.)

The question that we may want to ask ourselves is, have we made genuine efforts for reconciliation and peace? (Romans 12:18 Do all that you can to live in peace with everyone.) This scripture passage advises us to do all that WE can. There are times, despite all efforts,that the other individual is not receptive.

Sometimes relationships are ruined by holding on to unforgivness due to a particular offense. (Proverbs 10:12 Hatred stirs up quarrels, but love makes up for all offenses.)

The question between ourselves and God is - have we tried to forgive? Have we made attempts at peace? Are we possibly just going along with everybody else? How do we think Jesus would view our thinking and behavior.

At times, despite all attempts, discord remains. But we do not know if reconciliation is possible until we seek direction from God and make sincere efforts for peace.

Unbridled Faithfulness

Psalm 117

1 Praise the Lord, all you nations. Praise him, all you people of the earth.

2 For he loves us with unfailing love; the Lord's faithfulness endures forever. Praise the Lord!

The Lord is always worthy of praise, in whatever situation we face be it seemingly good or bad. Out of many difficult situations God is glorified and our faith is increased as He loves us with His unfailing love.

John 9:1-3, 6-7 1As Jesus was walking along, he saw a man who had been blind from birth. 2 "Rabbi," his disciples asked him, "why was this man born blind? Was it because of his own sins or his parents' sins?" 3 "It was not because of his sins or his parents' sins," Jesus answered. "This happened so the power of God could be seen in him. 6 Then he spit on the ground, made mud with the saliva, and spread the mud over the blind man's eyes. 7 He told him, "Go wash yourself in the pool of Siloam" (Siloam means "sent"). So the man went and washed and came back seeing!

I do not remember when I first read this passage from John chapter 9. I remember being amazed that God would allow blindness for His glorification. But lest we forget, this time on earth is to share the Good News of salvation. Our time on earth is brief compared with our eternal homes in heaven with Jesus. The Lord reminds us that our time on earth is to be about kingdom business. Yet in the midst of these difficulties and trials, God remains faithful. The man that was blind could now see. How much more would he appreciate his sight than those who were born seeing. How many people would be amazed at this miracle and want to talk about the Lord, where a seed could be planted and even some who would immediately give their lives over to Christ.

God is faithful in every circumstance. He is true to His word. He never leaves us or forsakes us and He never leaves us comfortless. At times His ways may seem peculiar to us, but He told us in His Word that this would be the case. (Isaiah 55:8-9 8 "My thoughts are nothing like your thoughts," says the Lord. "And my ways are far beyond anything you could imagine. 9 For just as the heavens are higher than the earth, so my ways are higher than your ways and my thoughts higher than your thoughts.)

Despite our understanding or our lack thereof, He has promised not that every situation would work for our good but He told us that God causes everything to work TOGETHER for the good of those who love God and are called according to his purpose for them. Romans 8:28.

Lord, thank you for your unbridled faithfulness.

Prepared To Share

Acts 2:41 Those who believed what Peter said were baptized and added to the church that day—about 3,000 in all.

Can we imagine 3000 people being saved in one day? It is a little hard to imagine. There is such overwhelming joy when people accept Jesus as their personal Savior. How could this have been possible? Did 3000 people come to the temple? The Word of God says that Peter was preaching to a crowd.(Acts 2:14).

Do we preach the gospel to crowds? Do we share the gospel with individuals? Do we go to people with the Word of God or are we waiting for the people to walk through the church doors, hearing the sermon and then accepting Christ as their Savior?

With what tenacity do we share the gospel? Some of us may be searching for that perfect moment when we can share the Word with someone. That moment may never come. Sharing the gospel can require that we move out of our comfort zone. With determination and a heart for God, we must be persistent in our efforts to share the gospel. If the people do not come in the church doors to be saved, it would seem that when we leave the church edifice that we would tell others about Jesus Christ with great tenacity.

2 Timothy 4:2 Preach the word of God. Be prepared, whether the time is favorable or not. Patiently correct, rebuke, and encourage your people with good teaching.

Mustard Seed Faith

Matthew 17:20 "You don't have enough faith," Jesus told them. "I tell you the truth, if you had faith even as small as a mustard seed, you could say to this mountain, 'Move from here to there,' and it would move. Nothing would be impossible."

Hebrews 11:1 11 Now faith is the substance of things hoped for, the evidence of things not seen.

We do not have to hope for what we already see. We must stand in faith when we cannot see what is ahead of us. We need faith when we stand in a desperate situation with seemingly no hope. Our God is not limited. He increases our faith as we stand in belief of the impossible. Have we ever faced an impossible situation, or at least one that appeared to be impossible? If we focus on the report we are given or the bank account balance or the sickness we or others have, we could spend much of our life being distraught.

We serve a God that is limited by nothing. He can not fail. We must pray and believe. He answers prayers. He is completely wise, so when the seemingly impossible manifests itself as possible, our faith increases and we know that no one could have done this but the Almighty God. There are times when He does not answer our prayers in the way we asked and we feel disappointed. But these are times when we must continue to stand in faith, knowing that whatever way He handled the situation is correct. Our God does not err, does not make mistakes, and is not surprised or confounded by the situations we face. He is always worthy of our trust.

If we have mustard seed faith, we could tell an actual mountain to move and it would. But if our faith has not yet grown to the size of a mustard seed, we can still stand on the faith that we have knowing that God is faithful and He will answer in the way that is best. Hold onto your faith. Do not give up. God is in the midst of every situation that you face.

John 14:18 I will not leave you comfortless: I will come to you.

Blameless Suffering

Job 1:1

1 There once was a man named Job who lived in the land of Uz. He was blameless—a man of complete integrity. He feared God and stayed away from evil.

When we read this first verse at the very beginning of the book of Job, we probably think, wow, what a great guy. He was blameless and stayed away from everything evil. Based on our own perceptions and insights, and if we are unaware of the story of Job, we would anticipate that this book is about a man who had a life where everything went his way. When you do not do anything wrong shouldn't everything go your way??? Well, not according to the word.

(John 16:33 33 I have told you all this so that you may have peace in me. Here on earth you will have many trials and sorrows. But take heart, because I have overcome the world.").

Job was presented by God to satan as a man who was full of integrity and that would follow God faithfully. Well satan countered this by saying Job was faithful because God gave him everything that he wanted. So God allowed satan to hurt job in many ways, with one stipulation, that satan could not take Job's life. We read where all of Job's children died,he lost all of his wealth, and he became incredibly sick to the point that when his friends came to see him they could barely recognize him. (Job 2:12-13 When they saw Job from a distance, they scarcely recognized him. Wailing loudly, they tore their robes and threw dust into the air over their heads to show their grief. 13 Then they sat on the ground with him for seven days and nights. No one said a word to Job, for they saw that his suffering was too great for words.)

Sometimes we are going through great and, seemingly endless suffering. We and those around us are trying to determine what we did wrong. The thought being that this horrendous trial would not have occurred except for punishment for some sin(s). But the book of Job clearly shows us something different. God was allowing Job to experience these things because of his faithfulness and to prove that his character would remain the same regardless of the circumstances in his life.

Job did remain faithful and he suffered greatly for a while. Although we are sometimes suffering as a result of what we have done, our difficulties could have arisen because of our faithfulness. The Lord may have said to satan, have you seen my servant _____ (place your name there.) He is faithful in all his dealings regardless of his circumstances.

GUARD YOUR HEART

Proverbs 4:23 Guard your heart above all else, for it determines the course of your life.

I imagine that most people have had the experience when we knew what was wrong or right in our minds. Yet our hearts told us something else, leaving us torn between logic and feeling.

How do we guard our hearts? One thing to do is to not be quick to expose our hearts. Sharing the feelings in our hearts prematurely or openly with others can leave us in a vulnerable state, of which some people will take advantage. If we give our hearts to Jesus, it will have a substantial impact on the course of our lives, If we leave our hearts unguarded, we may find that our course of life does not line up with the Lord's plan for us.

Psalm 139:16 You saw me before I was born. Every day of my life was recorded in your book. Every moment was laid out before a single day had passed.

A Clean Heart

Mark 7:14-15 Then Jesus called to the crowd to come and hear. "All of you listen," he said, "and try to understand. 15 It's not what goes into your body that defiles you; you are defiled by what comes from your heart.

Have you ever had a thought in your head, heard it, and then were amazed that felt that way about something or someone? We do not always realize was is lurking in our hearts.

Sometimes we do not realize that we have ill will against someone until we see them, especially if we have not seen them in a while. I have heard myself say in my head, "They make me sick". It is like a wow moment for me because I try very hard to forgive. It is the Godly thing to do and also because unforgiveness impacts our relationship with Christ. Though it is my desire to forgive, I am not always successful and have to ask the Lord to help me to forgive. He is so awesome. When He changes something in me there are times that I want to ask, how did you do that? But He is God. Nothing is too hard for Him.

Psalm 51:10

Create in me a clean heart, O God; and renew a right spirit within me.

Sincerity

Have you ever seen another believer who seemed way off track, in our opinion? They seemed one way in church and you happened to see them outside of church they were acting like a totally different person. What is our inclination when we see something like that? Is it to preach at the individual? Could we not wait for prayer meeting so that we could use their name aloud in prayer and verbalize the person's business or run to share on the phone with others the faults of this individual? Or might our behavior have been similar to that of Daniel's? Daniel was faithfully following God but many of his people were not. What did Daniel do? He interceded in prayer.

(Daniel 9:2-5 During the first year of his reign, I, Daniel, learned from reading the word of the Lord, as revealed to Jeremiah the prophet, that Jerusalem must lie desolate for seventy years. 3 So I turned to the Lord God and pleaded with him in prayer and fasting. I also wore rough burlap and sprinkled myself with ashes. 4 I prayed to the Lord my God and confessed: "O Lord, you are a great and awesome God! You always fulfill your covenant and keep your promises of unfailing love to those who love you and obey your commands. 5 But we have sinned and done wrong. We have rebelled against you and scorned your commands and regulations.)

This is just the beginning portion of the prayer. He prays a heart wrenching prayer for His people. Daniel set a great example for us in Daniel chapter 9. Are we, too, committed to doing what Daniel did? Rather than rushing to tell others about someone else's shortcomings, might we take it in sincere heart and mind to the Lord in prayer.

God Knows Us Best

Have you ever thought or heard someone say, I know myself better than anyone else? We may think so, but it is not true. God knows us better than we know ourselves. Have you ever been surprised at your response to something or the lack thereof? It is so important to pray before we make decisions and to pray before we do just about anything as we often do not know what we would do until a situation occurs.

A great example of this is found is the scripture passages below.

Matthew 26:31-35, 74-75

31 On the way, Jesus told them, "Tonight all of you will desert me. For the Scriptures say,

'God will strike the Shepherd, and the sheep of the flock will be scattered.'

32 But after I have been raised from the dead, I will go ahead of you to Galilee and meet you there."

33 Peter declared, "Even if everyone else deserts you, I will never desert you."

34 Jesus replied, "I tell you the truth, Peter—this very night, before the rooster crows, you will deny three times that you even know me."

35 "No!" Peter insisted. "Even if I have to die with you, I will never deny you!" And all the other disciples vowed the same.

74 Peter swore, "A curse on me if I'm lying—I don't know the man!" And immediately the rooster crowed.(Peter's third time denying Jesus)

75 Suddenly, Jesus' words flashed through Peter's mind: "Before the rooster crows, you will deny three times that you even know me." And he went away, weeping bitterly.

SEEK HIS DIRECTION

As believers we seek the Lord's direction often. Without His direction, how would we know how to deal with all of the challenges in this life? If, in seeking the Lord's guidance, we think we have heard an answer that does not line up with the Bible, the true and living Word of God; it is very likely that we misunderstood. It could be that we want Him to answer a certain way so much that we believe it is Him telling us what we want to hear. At other times there is so much confusion going on at the time that we are not still enough to hear.

The devil often tries to confuse the believer with lies as he is the father of lies (John 8:44). When I think of asking God how to handle a situation I am reminded of Jesus in the Garden of Gethsemane. He knew the horrific things that He was going to experience prior to His death. I imagine that He hoped that God would say, "Yes, there is another way to achieve my purpose." But this was the only way. Jesus alone could be the perfect sacrifice. How difficult it must have been to say, "Not my will but yours be done." (Matthew 26:39 He went on a little farther and bowed with his face to the ground, praying, "My Father! If it is possible, let this cup of suffering be taken away from me. Yet I want your will to be done, not mine.") We may not always receive the answer that we want from the Lord, but we know that whatever God says is pure. loving and true.

NEVER SAID NO

What if God never said, "No.". What if He gave us everything we asked for whenever we asked for it. If He did that, why would we need God? God is wiser, stronger, has more knowledge and awareness of the impact of decisions than anyone. That is one of the many reasons that we need God. We need His direction and guidance. Without it we could all go astray.

MIGHTY GOD

What an awesome God we serve! Who but He could do the miraculous things that He does. He created the earth in six days and rested on the 7th. He faithfully shows us the sun in the day and the moon at night. He made us with hearts and lungs that work continuously without effort on our part. He gave us the ability to speak so that we may proclaim His great and Holy name! He comforts us when there seems to be no comfort. He grants us peace in difficult situations, so calming we cannot understand. He is the mighty God we serve!

Even Greater Works

John 14:12 "I tell you the truth, anyone who believes in me will do the same works I have done, and even greater works, because I am going to be with the Father." (Jesus speaking) It is so amazing when we think about all that the Lord has done in our lives and specifically what He did that we can read about in the Bible. It is amazing to think that believers will do the same works as He and even greater works! I find that to be mind blowing. Do we believe that the above statement from Jesus is possible in our lives as believers? Do we trust Him that much? Let's not just look for little things. Let us seek the fullness of Jesus' statement to be manifest in our lives. Glory to God.

Alive!

I lost a family member last month. Probably that is poor choice of words because I know where they are. I was trying to understand something about myself and I did not notice it until yesterday. If the words passed away were used, I was OK. But if the word death was used, it upset me. Then God brought something he had said to me to my remembrance. He said that when this loved one passed, they would begin to live again. This earthly body had begun to greatly inhibit them. Once they were free of that old body that was wasting away, then he would be alive. So in my mind I picture this individual smiling and laughing and seeing our Savior, something that could never happen in this dying world. Death, where is thy sting? Jesus took away the sting of death when He died and rose again. My loved one is very much alive. Praise God!

Hanging On

Are you hanging on tightly to this life?

Mark 8:35 If you try to hang on to your life, you will lose it. But if you give up your life for my sake and for the sake of the Good News, you will save it.

Our anticipated length of life is approximately 70 years. (Psalm 90:10). Believers will live eternally with the Lord. Eternity does not have a number because it is never ending. But for purposes of this illustration, we will call eternity a 100,000 years. The percentage of time that we have on earth (70 years) compared to 100,000 is 0.07%. The non-percentage # is 0.0007.

We can get so caught up in the things of this world, worried, frantic, feeling like whatever the problem is will never end. That is understandable. This world is not our home, we are just strangers passing through. (Hebrews 13:14) Strangers may feel uncomfortable at times. But it is important that we remember that our time on earth is extremely short compared to living in our home in heaven. Whatever we are experiencing right now - it is truly temporary.

CLARITY

I remember years ago back in school I was riding mass transit. Talking with someone while riding was a good time to witness and it also helped the time to pass more quickly. I was talking about God, and in retrospect that word was too generic, as when I am talking about God, I mean our Lord and Savior. Well the lady I was speaking with said, yes we are all our own gods. In my head I said, "Whoa we are definitely NOT talking about the same thing." I tried then to talk about Jesus but she had already shut me out from a conversational standpoint.

I learned a couple of things that morning:

1. Be clear who you are speaking about when you are speaking about our Lord and Savior Jesus Christ.

2. Also, you cannot argue people into believing about Christ. It is a faith journey. I was not actually arguing with her but in order to share I should have listened to what she had to say as well, even though I did not believe it. Would you want to listen to someone who did not want to listen to you?

Hold On

Hold on. Are you having a hard time in your life? Hold on. Have you prayed and prayed and prayed and the situation still appears to be the same. Hold on. Do you feel like you cannot take this craziness one more day. Hold on. Are you crying out to Jesus but He does not seem to be hearing? Hold on. God hears, knows, and sees everything about us. He is working. It is sometimes difficult to stand your ground when you do not see anything. But that is when we have to use faith. He is working. He's got this. It may not work out the way you thought, but it will work together with other things for your good. Please hold on.

JESUS DIED FOR ALL

I would like to share an observation that I have noticed among believers. When we have sinned and fallen short of the glory of God, it has a tendency to remind us of what Jesus did on the cross, that incomparable sacrifice...and we are grateful, which is most appropriate. What I have noticed is that some of us forget that when Jesus went up on the cross He didn't leave anybody out. All sins were covered. We need only confess. Yet some people in the body of Christ will spend 10 - 20 years remembering what they perceive someone else did wrong. At times, it is not only remembered but shared. This is not what the Lord says for us to do. He did not pick and choose who and what was forgiven. He is not a respecter of persons. (Acts 10:34 & Romans 2:11) Repentance covers us all on the cross if we will accept it. Thank you Lord.

Who Is On First?

Who is on first? I believe that to originally be a baseball reference but it also applies well regarding our relationship with Christ. Sometimes in our zeal to serve the Lord we hurt others who we feel have not reached where we are or where we have determined that they should be. The example that we all are to follow is Jesus. We are not trying to emulate anyone else and we should not anticipate or have the expectation of someone trying to emulate us. Years ago, I wanted to go to a church where I felt very unwelcome due to some previous occurrences. I wanted to go to a funeral but was so apprehensive on the drive there that I started not to go. But I heard the Lord say, This is MY house and you are welcome. As far as who is on first, it should be the Lord for Christians. When we focus on what He says, it lessons the likelihood that we unintentionally (and definitely not intentionally) hurt others in the fellowship of Christ. The scripture reference is noted below.

Matthew 22:36-39

36 "Teacher, which is the most important commandment in the law of Moses?"

37 Jesus replied, "'You must love the Lord your God with all your heart, all your soul, and all your mind.' 38 This is the first and greatest commandment. 39 A second is equally important: 'Love your neighbor as yourself.'

RELATIONSHIP

Is anybody worth your relationship with God? There are people who have done and continue to do some rather awful things; things that we sometimes choose not to forgive. The Lord has said that if we do not forgive others, then He will not forgive us (Matthew 6:15). Our lack of forgiveness is not hurting the person that we haven't forgiven, it is hurting us. Whether the person chooses to receive it or not, their sins were also covered by the blood of Jesus. Some atrocities that people have committed make no sense and it is so incredibly difficult to get past the senselessness of what occurred. However, if we are holding on to these things we are impacting our relationship with Christ. And He understands how difficult it is to deal with what has been done. Let's pray now for anyone who is storing forgiveness in their heart, that they might ask God to help them forgive. When we pray in accordance with God's will, we know that He will answer us.

John 15:7 But if you remain in me and my words remain in you, you may ask for anything you want, and it will be granted!

Awesome God

How awesome is our God? When we look back over our lives and remember what he has brought us through in the past and even right now, isn't it amazing?! I remember some times in my life when I knew in my heart that God was able but my head (with my logical personality) could not determine how. I think today, how could I even think that I would know how God would handle a situation. Our almighty God is not limited in any way. He is not restricted where we see restrictions. He does things that we do not have the capacity to think or imagine. What a mighty God we serve!

UNCONDITIONAL

When we celebrate the resurrection of our Lord and Savior Jesus Christ, I continue to be amazed at the agape (unconditional) love shown towards us. Can we even imagine the pain and agony that our Lord suffered for us - knowing how often we would fail Him? Do we think of the incomparable sacrifice God gave in order for us to be able to commune with Him. I still marvel at this and cannot begin to explain how much I do not deserve this because of all of my shortcomings. Yet he keeps on loving me (us). Glory to God!

WELCOME ALL

Are we willing to overlook some things? Are we willing to not judge the appearance of a person so intently or look at them with such scorn that a person can come to church not looking "churchy"? That outfit may be the best that individual has.

Might we consider overlooking a strong alcohol smell or some other pungent odor long enough to share the gospel of Christ or not impede their ability to receive it with our judgment or looks of disdain? Years ago a friend of mine and her mother had planned to attend a church service at a church they had never attended. Although she and her mother favor each other in looks, it was clear that mother and daughter were not the same race. My friend told me that as they waited in the vestibule before entering the sanctuary, someone told them, "We don't have any of that here" and sent them away. I wondered if that church had allowed Jesus to enter?

Too Late

Noah's Ark. At that time people had not seen rain. I can imagine the people laughing and making fun of Noah. But when Noah had his family and all of the animals in the boat and the rain began, it was too late for the people outside of the Ark.

We know Jesus is coming back again. We do not want the unsaved to be longingly wishing that they had accepted Christ much as I imagine the people wanted to be inside the Ark when the rain began in Noah's day. We must share the gospel in word and deed so that others will know the awesome grace of salvation.

WE LOVE YOU

Christianity is not a bunch of rules to follow and restrictions that makes our lives dull, as some people perceive it. It is exciting when we think of the great love that our Heavenly Father had for us to allow His only begotten son to die on the cross for us. He loved us knowing all of our shortcomings, providing the ultimate sacrifice so that we can commune with Him. That is super exciting! Then we want to please Him out of sincere faith and gratitude for the salvation that was given that we absolutely do not deserve. We love you Lord.

OUR THOUGHTS

Something that was pointed out to me years ago by someone and something God periodically reminds me of is this: He hears what we are thinking. As believers we are hopefully paying attention to all of our communications, speaking, writing, non-verbals. These are all a reflection of Christ to nonbelievers and they definitely watch those who profess his name. But have we considered that God also hears what we are thinking?

THE ANGRY

It is a wonderful blessing to be able to pray silently as there are some situations where it is just not feasible to pray out loud.

Have you ever noticed that our thoughts are impacted by what we hear? If we are around a lot of cursing, curse words tend to come to mind. If we are around people that are angry often, there is that tendency to pick up the anger as well. This is at least worth pondering.

Proverbs 22:24-25 Don't befriend angry people or associate with hot-tempered people, 25 or you will learn to be like them and endanger your soul.

FRIEND TO OUTCASTS

Since Jesus was a friend to those who were considered outcasts; shouldn't we also do the same - while utilizing discernment and wisdom.

Luke 7:36-39

36 One of the Pharisees asked Jesus to have dinner with him, so Jesus went to his home and sat down to eat. 37 When a certain immoral woman from that city heard he was eating there, she brought a beautiful alabaster jar filled with expensive perfume. 38 Then she knelt behind him at his feet, weeping. Her tears fell on his feet, and she wiped them off with her hair. Then she kept kissing his feet and putting perfume on them.

39 When the Pharisee who had invited him saw this, he said to himself, "If this man were a prophet, he would know what kind of woman is touching him. She's a sinner!

Not Lukewarm

Have you ever experienced a very hot day and longed for some really cold water? Have you ever been subjected to a really cold day and couldn't wait until you got some hot coffee, tea, or hot chocolate? In either scenario, the hot or cold day, what if the liquid that you got was just lukewarm - not cold enough to cool you or hot enough to warm you? I propose that we would throw it out. It would not meet the need we were seeking. Are we lukewarm in our stance for God and how we live our life for God? The word says that the lukewarm would be spit out. Which are we choosing to be today and henceforth?

Revelation 3:15-17 Words to the Church in Laodicea

15 "I know all the things you do, that you are neither hot nor cold. I wish that you were one or the other! 16 But since you are like lukewarm water, neither hot nor cold, I will spit you out of my mouth! 17 You say, 'I am rich. I have everything I want. I don't need a thing!' And you don't realize that you are wretched and miserable and poor and blind and naked.

Endure For Christ

When I read this testimony of Paul's below, it leads me to ponder many things. Look at all that Paul was willing to endure for Christ in order to share the gospel. When spoken to in an evil manner, he responds in kindness. That in and of itself is a witness as it baffles people. Sometimes that will prompt people to ask you, why are you not saying or doing anything (as you are being spoken to or treated cruelly?)

1 Corinthians 4:11-13

11 To this hour we are hungry and thirsty, and our clothes are worn out. People hurt us. We have no homes.

12 We work with our hands to make a living. We speak kind words to those who speak against us. When people hurt us, we say nothing. 13 When people say bad things about us, we answer with kind words. People think of us as dirt that is worth nothing and as the worst thing on earth to this day.

BLESSED

Numbers 22:12 But God told Balaam, "Do not go with them. You are not to curse these people, for they have been blessed!" When God blesses us with something, there is almost always somebody that has some negativity about it. But what God has blessed cannot be cursed. If you are familiar with this passage, Balaam eventually goes to the place where Balaak wanted the Israelites to be cursed. But instead, God had Balaam speak more blessings over his people and spoke curses over Balaak and his people. Balaam had told Balaak, I can only say what God tells me to say. People may try but they do not have a chance when they try to curse those whom God has blessed. Romans 8:31 What shall we say about such wonderful things as these? If God is for us, who can ever be against us?

IT HAPPENED

Have you ever been going through a particularly difficult trial and you know the answer is in Jesus. There is absolutely nothing that you can do. Have you then given it to God and said, "Lord, please have your way"? After that, the thing you were most concerned about happening did actually happen. This is often followed by frustrating feelings. Gratefully, God understands that. At some later time we may understand but the truth is we may never understand. God is sovereign, having supreme rank and authority. He is also infallible, absolutely trustworthy, sure and impossible of error. Sometimes things that occur in this world can leave us perplexed; feeling heart wrenched. But the Lord who made the heavens and the earth is always right. Sometimes I have to remind myself of this scripture that I hope also helps you. 1 Chronicles 29:15 We are here for only a moment, visitors and strangers in the land as our ancestors were before us. Our days on earth are like a passing shadow, gone so soon without a trace. Our eternal home will be with the Lord. We have to trust and have faith - even when we do not understand.

Trust Him

Psalm 55:16-19, 22

16 But I will call on God,
and the Lord will rescue me.

17 Morning, noon, and night
I cry out in my distress,
and the Lord hears my voice.

18 He ransoms me and keeps me safe
from the battle waged against me,
though many still oppose me.

19 God, who has ruled forever,
will hear me and humble them. Interlude
For my enemies refuse to change their ways;
they do not fear God.

22 Give your burdens to the Lord,
and he will take care of you.
He will not permit the godly to slip and fall.

No matter what the type of battle: illness, bereavement, finances,
difficult people, job loss, etc - give your burden to the Lord. HE
WILL answer. HE WILL take care you. TRUST HIM.

THANKS

God is so good. Sometimes the trials we go through are tough. But what if God allowed everything to go our way all the time and then a catastrophic or just a difficult thing came our way. If we hadn't been through anything before, we would probably fall apart. Thank you Lord for the trials. You ALWAYS know what we need.

It Won't Last

I had surgery 2 days ago. I didn't realize how much pain medicine the doctor had put into the surgery site until 24 hours passed and it wore off. Wow - pain. But it helped me to remember what life is really like. To get where God wants us to be, there can be considerable pain, but that is not the end for believers.

Isaiah 33:6 In that day he will be your sure foundation, providing a rich store of salvation, wisdom, and knowledge. The fear of the Lord will be your treasure.

I know that I am hurting now, but it won't last. For those who are suffering pain now of any sort, please know that it will also not last.

John 16:33 I have told you all this so that you may have peace in me. Here on earth you will have many trials and sorrows. But take heart, because I have overcome the world."

GOD HELPED ME

May I ask, has reality ever smacked you in the face? I got a little dose of that today. There was something that was wrong and I have known it for a while. I think I had pushed it out of my mind so I didn't have to deal with it. The matter came up today and it threw me off kilter for a while. But God helped me.

Enthusiastic Work

Many times on television I have seen local colleges advertising their certified nurses aides program. The commercials make this position appear alluring and enjoyable. This is not my occupational field but I have great respect for those who have this position and put effort into doing it well. I think these individuals are often underappreciated.

Over the past nine years, I have visited quite a few nursing homes due to ill relatives, church members, or acquaintances. From what I can see, being a nurses aide is a difficult and often strenuous position that may require some unglamorous activities. I have seen situations when people needed assistance and there was no one around or there was apparent irritation at the request of helping with toileting, bathing and such. In a field where people are reliant on you for basic living needs, if one finds that they hate doing this job might I request that you seek another occupation. Whether or not one enjoys doing the job, the needs of the ill individual remain. As Christians we are to do our work as unto the Lord.

Ephesians 6:7 Work with enthusiasm, as though you were working for the Lord rather than for people.

GOD-PLANNED STEPS

Life is interesting. This time last year I was walking fine - although I was aware that I had arthritis and bursitis in both knees. Later in the year, the left knee began to give me significant problems and needed to have arthroscopic surgery. By the grace of God there was substantial improvement. While my left knee was healing I tended to put more weight on my right knee and subsequently I started having significant problems with it too. Surgery is now being planned for that knee. From a Christian spiritual standpoint there is a bit that the Lord showed me from this situation. First, when something is difficult, we should put our weight and trust in Him. Secondly, there may be steps that we have to take in order to reach the point where God is taking us. The surgery is outpatient and I will need some healing time but it is necessary to reach the goal. At times when we are having problems and it seems that things are getting even worse, we need to remember that we often have to take God-planned steps in order to achieve His goal.

PEACEFUL STREAMS

Sometimes life seems crazy. At times we come across problems that are perplexing and stressful and at times, we just do not know what to do. This morning I was reading my Bible and came across Psalm 23. I am very familiar with that passage. However, sometimes our perceived familiarity allows us to overlook things. Here is what stood out to me at this time that had not stood out to me before: God let's us rest and then He guides us through in peace. Psalm 23:2 2 He lets me rest in green meadows; he leads me beside peaceful streams.

That is so comforting.

WHEN TO PRAISE

When is it a good time to praise God? Praise God when we are happy and when we are sad. Praise God when everything is going our way and when everything seems to be going against us. Praise Him when we are healthy and praise Him when we are ill. Praise Him when our eyes open in the morning and when we can taste and swallow our food. Praise Him when our muscles are working properly. Praise Him when we can pay the bills and praise Him when it seems that we can't. Whatever is happening, we are to praise Him as we know that all these things are working together for our good.

Romans 8:28 And we know that all things work together for good to them that love God, to them who are the called according to his purpose.

HURTING OTHERS

I am going to be totally transparent. I generally do not share my strong feelings about things except with those whom I am very close. The body of Christ - not a particular church or denomination - just Christians, followers of Christ. I am not speaking of all, but I am definitely speaking of some. I wonder why, and I have seen this O so many times, we hurt each other. Christians will lie about one another. (Exodus 20:16 "You must not testify falsely against your neighbor.) Believers will gossip about one another or listen to gossip, sometimes on the pretext of someone needing prayer but knowing inside that their is a deep desire to tell what someone else did wrong. (Psalm 41:6 They visit me as if they were my friends, but all the while they gather gossip, and when they leave, they spread it everywhere. Proverbs 16:28 A troublemaker plants seeds of strife; gossip separates the best of friends. Proverbs 17:4 WRONGDOERS eagerly listen to gossip; liars pay close attention to slander. Proverbs 25:10 Others may accuse you of gossip, and you will never regain your good reputation.) Some Christians believe that they have "arrived". People who have not reached "their level" are beneath them. Has anyone heard of pride? If by some chance any believer thinks they have everything together, which is EXTREMELY unlikely, then that person has an issue with pride. (Proverbs 16:18 Pride goes before destruction, and haughtiness before a fall. Psalm 59:12 Because of the sinful things they say, because of the evil that is on their lips, let them be captured by their pride, their curses, and their lies.) Some people in the body love to keep confusion going, creating disharmony among the brethren. (1 Corinthians 14:33 For God is not a God of disorder but of peace, as in all the meetings of God's holy people.) Do we truly love God and are we trying to live as he has taught? Look at the sacrifice that He made for us. Jesus asked His Father is there any other way that we can do this, as He knew the humiliation and agony required for him to be the perfect sacrifice. (Luke 22:42 "Father, if you are willing, please take this cup of suffering away from me. Yet I want your will to be done, not mine." John 8:7 They kept demanding an answer, so he stood up again and said, "All right, but let the one who has never sinned throw the first stone!") Dare any of us cast one stone? This may displease some people. However, we are on this earth to please GOD, not people.

Heed His Voice

The branch of the bank that was nearest to me had an ATM behind the building. I was driving up and I noticed a young man leaving the fast food establishment beside the bank. He was headed toward the street. When I pulled up to the ATM a voice in my head said, "Run". I looked in the rear view mirror and saw that the man who had been heading toward the street had changed his path and was headed over in my direction. I make no pretense of knowing what God is saying all of the time. But we need to be listening. Sometimes it can be a strong feeling that we are in a place that we do not need to be. Heed God's voice. By doing so, we may avoid many sorrows.

WE MUST FORGIVE

Not that long ago there were several people that I thought I knew because I had been around them in a limited capacity for years. Circumstances changed and I ended up being around them more and they were malicious towards me. For what reasons, I have no idea. No one came to me and said I offended them - as all parties are believers - and we are to go to another when we have issues with them according to the Bible. Sometimes God takes you through the situation and others times He tells you to get out of it. He told me to go. I am so grateful. But He (the Lord) reminded me that I need to forgive them. I haven't seem them for a few months now and pretty much have put them out of my mind; but as the Lord reminded me that is not the same thing as forgiveness. I asked God to help me forgive them as I really didn't even know what we (they) were upset about. So I am asking God for His help to forgive and so that He may be pleased with me. I hate to disappoint the Lord.

SHARE

I moved from one house to another a few years back. The second house was a little smaller so I was having some difficulty figuring out where to put my things. For a few months my dining room and living room, while orderly was filled to the point that it looked too full. Then it finally dawned on me (through God) that I should give some things away. The place would look much better. So I did. The house looked better and I knew that some other people received some nice things. Sometimes we hold onto someone else's blessings. If money is short - a garage sale or yard sale may be the best way to go. But if we have more than enough, why not share?

TREATMENT

A beloved family member has been ill for a while. Initially, we liked the first nursing facility where he was but then various issues arose and we knew that we needed to relocate them. The nursing home was going through a total remodel. That's when it became evident how unimportant the people were to the facility's management. Rather than have one hall completely done so that the patients had to move only once, people (some really ill people) were being moved 3 and 4 times. When my family member was moved 3 times within a two week period, we knew it was time to make a change.

This also reminded me of a company I worked for who would call groups of people into a meeting to tell them that this was there last day and to pack up their things. No warning at all. But I once saw a job posting that referred to people as "human capital". That perception of the employees was evident in how they treated us.

2 Timothy 3:2a For people will love only themselves and their money.

INVEST IN CHILDREN

Many times I have heard the phrase - "The children are our future". Well children are also in the present and what we do with them now shapes their future. Invest and instill in them Biblical values and knowledge along with a genuine respect for other people and the children will have a more promising future. While teachers and churches may assist in helping the development of the child, the ownership of this responsibility resides with the parents. To God be the glory!

Have We Asked?

About 10 years ago a friend of mine and I recalled how much fun we use to have at a well-known amusement park. We decided to go. I was so excited when we were buckling up to get on what was once the longest roller coaster in the US. Well the roller coaster went slowly up the big first hill and then it hit, we went slamming down the steep hill with my body being thrown in every direction. It was quite jarring and could not wait to get off of that roller coaster. My body was no longer up for taking that kind of abuse. I wondered why did I EVER think this was fun???? I had looked backwards and gone backwards. In retrospect, I do not remember asking the Lord what He thought of my plans. From a spiritual standpoint it is so easy to go back to where we were because it was a comfortable time; sometimes not taking the time to ask the Lord. Have we asked the Lord what He would have us doing right now in our spiritual walk?

Not Deserved

I am thankful that God is kind, loving, forgiving, a provider, teacher, guide, friend, deliverer and so much more. I do not deserve it, but you do it anyway. Thank you Lord.

PLANT AND HARVEST

One of my good friends and I went to a well-known restaurant chain. We had been there many times before as many of the workers recognize us when we arrive. On that particular day we had a new waitress. She was extremely slow, unfriendly and once we received our food she did not check on us even once. The only other thing she did was put the bill on the table and say, "Here's the bill". This eating establishment had one centralized place for all to pay, though as usual you would leave the tip on the table. We knew this type of service was not their norm and as we paid for our food, we spoke to the manager about it. Incredibly, the server found the way to our table very quickly once we got up. (I believe in 15% gratuity and 20% or a little more for exceptional service.) Each of us left her a quarter. When she saw the quarters she looked over and glared at us. Have you ever heard of self-fulfilling prophecy? Had the woman given us good service she would have received a good tip. Since she anticipated not getting a good tip - she gave service that did not warrant any tip. We left the quarters to make a point.

Galatians 6:7 Don't be misled—you cannot mock the justice of God. You will always harvest what you plant.

Do Not Judge

I frequently visit a beloved family member at a nursing facility. I used to wonder how people could let their loved ones live in a nursing home. It can be a gradual or a somewhat catastrophic illness that prompts this. Insurance will allow them to stay in the hospital for a determined length of time. After that, the insurance more or less says,"Get out". The hospital social worker will usually come talk to the family and advise of which nursing home has an opening and asks your preference of locations. It's so disheartening because you don't have the skill, knowledge base, physical capacity, or home design,etc to accommodate this individual that you love so very much. All too often in various situations we look from the outside of a situation and make our assessments when we lack sufficient knowledge to do so. I think that this may be one of the reasons that God told us not to judge. - Matthew 7:1 "Do not judge others, and you will not be judged.

"ME GENERATION"

I do not remember when I first heard this terminology - "The Me Generation". I think that people were so enthralled with "The Me Generation" that it never ended. As Christians these are not words that should be descriptive of us. Yes, we do matter. But our purpose on earth is to live for Christ, share Christ and care for one another. Philippians 2:3 Let nothing be done through strife or vainglory; but in lowliness of mind let each esteem other better than themselves.

Witness

This is something I don't think I will ever forget. Our church went out in teams to tell people about some activities going on in church. The person I was with was a good friend and she and I were both enjoying talking with people. We knocked on the door of one residence where the screen door was closed but the main door was open. A male who could see us sounded very happy to see us and asked us to please wait until he could put on proper attire for coming to the door. He soon smilingly approached the door. We started talking about Jesus and the church activities. His demeanor changed almost instantly and he said that he was too busy to talk. When we witness to others, their response is not our responsibility. Our responsibility is to share the Good News. Can we remember when we last witnessed to someone? Why not today?

WILL YOU BE READY

Recently I was driving home in the evening. It was before 8pm, but at this time of year it gets dark very early. I was driving around the bend when I saw a car pull up to a stop sign but as I continued driving they did not move. There were no houses at the end of that street, so I did not think they were waiting on anyone. So I slowed down but kept moving and when they continued to sit I decided to pass my street and not go home yet. Interestingly, when I drove slowly past the street of my residence I could see in my rear view mirror that they turned around. I believe they knew where I was going and when I did not turn onto my street, they realized that I was very aware of them. Thank you Lord for protection.

The word of God at 1 Thessalonians 5:2 says:

For you know quite well that the day of the Lord's return will come unexpectedly, like a thief in the night.

When the Lord returns will you be ready. Will you have accepted Jesus as your Savior?

No Lemons

There is an old saying that when life you gives you lemons, make lemonade. But to alter that a bit, before you eat any lemons or drink any lemonade call on Jesus.

TEMPTATION

Friday nights. They can be very difficult for single people. (Please note that this message is for females and males. God did not create different rules for being sexually moral based on gender.) It can be difficult for singles due to not having a date, difficulty interacting with their date in a Godly fashion, and/or guilt for what activities that individual engaged in while with their date. God created some people with singleness in mind or marriage later in life. Some have to fight the battle knowing that our bodies are the temple of the Holy Ghost, recognizing that we may "lose" our date if we interact with our date only in the ways that God said. Others are engaged in consistently immoral activity. The activity is only immoral if the pair is unmarried. The marriage bed is blessed and conjugal activity is a gift for those who are married. Difficult situations need to be handed over to the Lord. God's guidelines have not changed. When we tell God that we want to live life His way, are we willing to include abstinence unless/until married?

1 Corinthians 10:13

The temptations in your life are no different from what others experience. And God is faithful. He will not allow the temptation to be more than you can stand. When you are tempted, he will show you a way out so that you can endure.

TAKEN FOR GRANTED

Quite a few years back, I left work and headed home. It seemed every street light was red, then I had to wait for a train. I avoided the highway due to construction. Then I had a car accident. It was not deemed my fault but I was quite upset. I was not injured. I remember initially being frustrated with the Lord, thinking that if there had not been so many red lights and the train I would have missed being in the accident. But God reminded me of all the times that I driven to and from work and had NOT had an accident. Had I even thought about thanking him for that? I honestly do not think so. Thank you Lord for keeping me safe and please forgive me for all of the things that you have done for me that I have taken for granted. I love you Lord.

EVERY GIFT

I am remembering a Sunday School class from years ago when we were talking about the body of Christ and being appreciative of others. Someone mentioned the preacher and people started talking about taking the preacher to dinner. Then someone mentioned the custodian and people started mentioning that he didn't leave enough toilet tissue in the restroom and some areas on the floor that were not being cleaned well enough. I do believe the position of the custodian was devalued. Definitely no one was talking about taking him to dinner or recognizing his efforts. - Years ago I lived next door to a man who was missing his big toe on one foot, and that had a significant impact on his walking. I mention that to say the prominent parts of the body as well as the tiny ones are important in the body of Christ. Let's appreciate, not compete, and praise God for the gifts and talents within the body of Christ.

1 Corinthians 12:7 A spiritual gift is given to each of us so we can help each other.

MOST IMPORTANT

The most important thing you can receive is salvation. The most precious thing you can receive is a personal relationship with Jesus Christ.

Made In His Image

I have heard people marvel at snow flakes saying that no two are exactly the same. But what about people? With two eyes, one nose, two ears, one mouth and different shading, we look different. Who could do anything like that but our mighty God?

Psalm 8:4

What is man, that thou art mindful of him? and the son of man, that thou visitest him?

Genesis 9:6b

For God made human beings in his own image.

MIRACLES

I have taken up a new hobby - photography. I love it; and I have noticed that when I am keeping an eye out for a great photo shot, I am more aware of the beauty of God's creations. God's created miracles are all around us. Just another great reason to give him thanks. Praise God!

In Harmony

One of the most exciting things in the world is when someone accepts Christ as their Lord and Savior. This is often seen at church. Sometimes church members change their membership to our particular church of attendance and we welcome them with open arms, hopefully. But every Bible believing church is just a portion of the body of Christ. All believers as a whole make up the body.

Observation: as happy as we are when we someone comes from another fellowship, there seems to be feelings of animosity when someone leaves our fellowship to go to another. As long as the person is still following Christ, can we find a way not to harbor animosity towards them. God gives people assignments using the gifts he has given each individual as He sees fit. Sometimes, one place is training ground. Other times there is a need at another church that is fulfilled at the fellowship from which one came.

Psalm 133:1 How wonderful and pleasant it is when brothers live together in harmony! If we are hurt by the departure of someone from the church - and the people are the church - we are the temple of the Holy Ghost. (1 Corinthians 6:19), why not pray to God about it. He loves it when His children reconcile with one another!

HEAVEN!

Do you ever think about Heaven? What a blessing to bow at our Savior's feet, to walk with Him, talk with Him, maybe fly with Him or swim with Him. Just to see His face, the thought is overwhelming knowing His incomparably loving sacrifice. We will also get to see loved ones that have gone before us. What a day of rejoicing that will be!

God's Protection

A couple of weeks ago I had a flat tire. I didn't realize at first why my car was sounding a little funny. But the sound got louder so I got out of the car to look and saw that the tire was almost completely flat and it would not have been wise to continue driving. That could have damaged the wheel and the car's alignment. Life happens but I was a little frustrated waiting for the truck to come and put on my spare tire. After the tire had been changed and I headed to my destination I saw something I had never seen before as the police had closed off one side of the street. The police were there with a covered body pulled to the side of the street with only shoes protruding from under the covering. We know from Psalm 139 that God established all of our days before we began to breathe, so it must have been the day that the Lord decided that this individual should come home. However, the Lord spoke to me in a still, small voice as I drove and looked over in shock, " If not for the flat tire, you would have been the one that hit and killed this man". Sometimes there is a reason that we cannot get where we want to go at the time that we want. God is protecting us.

Too Hard

Is anything too hard for God???? - Luke 1:37

For nothing is impossible with God."

SHIFTS

Shifts. There is a place that I frequent that has a crazy elevator which will drop down (not a whole floor) before it heads up to the floor I want as I would have pushed the up button. Sometimes the bounce is more intense than others and I get a little nervous. That can happen when the Lord is making shifts in our lives. It seems like we are going down, and it's uncomfortable for a little bit. In the Bible Jesus, Abraham, David, Paul, etc. were often on the move. A move doesn't have to be a bad thing. Sometimes God has to shake us up enough to get us from our comfortable position to where he wants us to be.

Call Or Visit

Let us not forget the lonely, depressed, sick, homeless, jobless, etc. They could probably use a call or visit today so that they know they are not forgotten. They may already know but it, but it may help them to hear it from someone else anyway.

Is It You?

Change often starts with only one person standing up against something wrong? Are you that person?

Vessel of Love

I remember when I was visiting a lady at a nursing home who was extremely ill. She was blind, had both legs amputated, could not help herself in anyway that I could tell. She was a Christian so when I came I would read the Bible to her. That is all that I knew to do as she didn't talk either. One day when I got to the nursing home, the lady's son was there. I do not know how to explain it as she was just as sick but she was glowing. She wasn't smiling, but she looked happy. I believe the immense love that she felt from her son brought about these changes. Do you know someone who is truly struggling? God is the problem solver and sometimes He allows us to be the vessel that He uses in people's situations. Let us be one of God's vessels of love.

PLEASING REACTION

What do we do? What is our first response? When something unpleasant or rude or thoughtless occurs, our first response can be to tell someone off, curse them out, call them a name that God did not give to one of His creations, fall apart, etc. It is very important that we give ourselves a minute or two to determine if our first response would be the right response. The right response would be Christlike. Would our response or reaction be one that pleases God?

All Sin

Something came to mind today that I think I should share. Sometimes we get involved in doing something that is ungodly. And it's like the more it's done the less guilt can be felt or we might feel less conviction from the Holy Spirit as time passes. Despite our feelings, God sees, hears and knows what we are and are not doing. My hypothesis is that He is giving us time to get it together before he lovingly disciplines us. The enemy will try and trick us into thinking that no one knows or that God doesn't really care while in actuality - God hates ALL sin.

OTHERS

Luke 3:11

11 John replied, "If you have two shirts, give one to the poor. If you have food, share it with those who are hungry."

How much do we care about other people? Sometimes we are unrecognized hoarders, not that our houses are filled to the brim with objects in every room. But when we choose not to give to the poor or the hungry when we know there is a need, we are hoarding what God gave us to share. Sometimes we are skeptical of people holding signs on the street asking for things, but we can contribute to groups or organizations that help the poor and hungry.

NOT DESERVED

Something that perplexes me - and maybe it is just because we have not really thought about what we are saying. Have you heard people say, "Jesus helped me even when I didn't deserve it". I'm trying to figure out when we ever deserved God's grace and mercy. The truth is that we NEVER deserved it. He just loved us enough to give it to us anyway.